Life of a Bubble

Life of a Bubble

A Collection of Short Poems

Hamid Mojdehi

RESOURCE *Publications* • Eugene, Oregon

LIFE OF A BUBBLE
A Collection of Short Poems

Copyright © 2021 Hamid Mojdehi. All rights reserved. Except for brief quotations in critical publications or reviews, no part of this book may be reproduced in any manner without prior written permission from the publisher. Write: Permissions, Wipf and Stock Publishers, 199 W. 8th Ave., Suite 3, Eugene, OR 97401.

Resource Publications
An Imprint of Wipf and Stock Publishers
199 W. 8th Ave., Suite 3
Eugene, OR 97401

www.wipfandstock.com

PAPERBACK ISBN: 978-1-6667-1565-1
HARDCOVER ISBN: 978-1-6667-1566-8
EBOOK ISBN: 978-1-6667-1567-5

JULY 7, 2021

*This book is dedicated to my wife Mahboubeh,
my son and daughter Komale and Samaneh,
their partners in life Hanieh and Alan,
and the two angels on my shoulders, Dion and Sophie.*

Contents

Preface | viii
Man and his Boat | 1
Wrongdoing | 2
Footprint | 3
Resting Place | 4
Home | 5
Treasure of Life | 6
Going Astray | 7
Burning Candle | 8
Empty Words | 9
Wisdom | 10
Creation | 11
All in the Mind | 12
Doubts | 13
Parents | 14
Sunshine | 15
Man's Journey | 16
Children | 17
A Sad Joke | 18
Power of Thought | 19
The Fool and the Wise | 20

Man's Punishment | 21
The Other Side | 22
Foolish Pride | 23
Desireless | 24
Man's Plight | 25
Friendship | 26
Pit of Darkness | 27
All the Lies | 28
Rain | 29
Life Without Hate | 30
Past Glory | 31
Changing Beliefs | 32
Ocean of Greed | 33
Hidden Flaws | 34
Prejudice | 35
Always There | 36
Personal Story | 37
Oblivion | 38
Light of Wisdom | 39
The End Game | 40
Rise Above | 41

What I Know | 42	Kindness | 71
Words and Jewels | 43	Life | 72
Dark Road | 44	Fool's Logic | 73
Peace | 45	Destiny's Game | 74
Ignorance | 46	Passengers | 75
No Borders | 47	Old Age | 76
Secret Potion | 48	Joy for All | 77
Aching Heart | 49	Changing World | 78
Life in Vain | 50	Wings of Wisdom | 79
Little Joys | 51	Poor and Rich | 80
Mirror to the Soul | 52	Blindness | 81
Deeds | 53	Power of Destiny | 82
Blind Devotion | 54	Man's Curiosity | 83
Coming to Disappear | 55	Slave's Prayer | 84
Pain of being Sober | 56	Hollow Words | 85
Rain of Wisdom | 57	Autumn Winds | 86
Understanding | 58	Faults | 87
Nothingness | 59	Picture on the Wall | 88
Regrets | 60	The Preacher | 89
Will | 61	Insignificance | 90
Friends | 62	God's Mold | 91
Hidden Faces | 63	Crying Man | 92
At the Heart | 64	Love the Living | 93
Masterful | 65	Light of Life | 94
Man and The Stars | 66	Generous Sun | 95
Inside | 67	Last Wish | 96
Art of Living | 68	My World | 97
Wine from Heaven | 69	Speck of Dust | 98
The Only Hand | 70	Joy of Others | 99

Life and Death | 100	Awakened Mind | 129
Imagination | 101	Divided | 130
Selfish Man | 102	Life of a Bubble | 131
Different God | 103	Secrets | 132
Clues | 104	Lonely Journey | 133
Struggle | 105	Troubled Heart | 134
Darkness | 106	Friend Indeed | 135
Destiny | 107	Autumn of Life | 136
Pure Joy | 108	To the Creator | 137
Dearly Departed | 109	Fear of Life | 138
Gone | 110	In Due Time | 139
My Eyes | 111	Man in the Frame | 140
Last Grasp | 112	At Peace | 141
Our Dust | 113	Last Kiss | 142
Secrets of Creation | 114	Death | 143
End of Life | 115	Taking Action | 144
Giving Life | 116	The Plan | 145
Purpose | 117	House of Dirt | 146
Greed | 118	True Friend | 147
Aimless | 119	Actions and Prayers | 148
Dark Journey | 120	New World | 149
Puzzle of Life | 121	Teaching by Action | 150
The Promise | 122	
The Wise | 123	
Words | 124	
Actions | 125	
Actions and Thoughts | 126	
Memories | 127	
Last Day | 128	

Preface

THIS BOOK IS WRITTEN for those who enjoy reading poetry about Man's life, its imagined purpose, the confusion inherent in it, and the ups and downs of our journey through it which inevitably culminates in death. The poems are inspired by the ancient Persian poet Omar Khayyam and his thoughts on life and death. They are easy to understand for all groups, whether laymen or professionals. If you have ever wondered about Man's creation and been bewildered by death and our struggle through life with understanding the logic behind it, this book is a thought-provoking collection of poems you will enjoy.

Man and his Boat

on the walls of this creation the almighty wrote

truly I created the world with good and bad, O' Man take a note

bestowed on Man part of my own supreme self

however, he keeps on doing wrong and sure missing the boat

Wrongdoing

Man is indeed born to do wrong

no way out, other than to learn and stay strong

wrongdoing is truly part of our being and this life

tragedy is when we keep on doing wrong and taking misery along

Footprint

any of us as we leave this life and go to the unknown

we sure leave a footprint of some sort on the face of this earth,
 the only thing we own

the best of such prints we can ever leave behind, remember

is when we guided a lost soul in need of the way to be shown

Resting Place

the ground you step on so firmly and proud

is the home to thousands of kings and queens who lived under the cloud

we will all end up in that same home of darkness, just remember

the last resting place for all men, remind everyone else aloud

Home

home is where you are at peace, happy and content

home is where there is no sign of anger or ill intent

if wherever you are offers you such qualities of life

that is your home, no matter where or on what continent

Treasure of Life

Man never treasures what he has, till it is taken away

like water and air, we don't realize the critical role they play

truly life is as such, unaware we go through the journey

when near the end, wonderful gifts of life are greatly missed, to our dismay

Going Astray

dear God, you have given Man the capacity to think

he is also given the power of learning and finding
   the missing link

sadly, he keeps going astray most of the time

is there anything else he should have been given, for his ship
   not to sink?

Burning Candle

see the candle giving light as it gradually dies

it sacrifices its being to brighten lives

O' friend, our good deeds are a source of light indeed

how miserable life is when there is only darkness for the eyes

Empty Words

these ears hear words of all sorts everyday

believing all you hear is not a wise game to play

Man utters words with no thought all the time

the wise takes words through many filters of thought, before setting them in clay

Wisdom

having wisdom there is no wrong to do

our life is much sweeter, pain and
suffering so few

all selfishness is gone, caring and
kindness for all to view

sorrow is replaced with joy, for me and you

Creation

O' dear God, tell us the secret only you hold

tell us your purpose for creation and this human mold

such delicate instruments you build so wonderful and bold

then breaking them one by one in an act so cold

All in the Mind

what we grow in our minds, that is who we are in life

with beautiful thoughts, then glorious we live, no strife

cleanse the mind of all your dark desires

how serene life is then for all, happiness so rife

Doubts

doubt and hesitation are the arsenals of the wise

he thinks through everything in detail, all he must revise

the fool never doubts, as his perceptions he thinks,
   are always right

this is what makes him a destructive force of nature, in disguise

Parents

see the baby sleeping peaceful and calm

at his corner, see that mountain of love, dad and mom, absorbed in his charm

sleepless nights they stare into the eyes of the child

the only thought they have is to keep his precious life away from any harm

Sunshine

like the Sun that shines equally on all beings on this earth

open your arms to all, irrespective of race or place of birth

aren't we all created from the same ocean of creation

why then, there is so much pain and suffering around our lonely earth

Man's Journey

listen to the sad story of Man and his journey

struggles his whole life for fame and fortune, crossing over many bridges of sorrow and worry

as he gets near the end, all wealth and power seem so insignificant indeed

when gone, see him carried to his grave with empty hands and a face so pale and sorry

Children

love of a child is the strongest love of all

you'll do anything in your power to keep them from a fall

be diligent so they grow up to be wise and free

otherwise, your life becomes a mountain of misery so wide and tall

A Sad Joke

life seems like a joke played on us all

don't bother looking for meaning and rationale at all

Man seems going around a circle till curtains fall

no one knows what happens when it all ends, big or small

Power of Thought

O' young man, don't be too proud of your youth and your powers

this fragile old man in front of you was also young, sturdy
   as towers

the pride of power and beauty will leave you very soon

the power of thought will last throughout your life and all your
   waking hours

The Fool and the Wise

the fool keeps making the same mistakes in life

all he builds are so skewed and misery is rife

he who yearns for wisdom keeps moving towards the light

makes his path straight and smooth, lives with little Strife

Man's Punishment

O' God of all the galaxies and all the stars

O' the creator of Man, Jupiter and Mars

you're the one who gave me all my shortcomings

why then, am I the one who is punished in your hell and left with all the scars

The Other Side

don't bother waiting for news from the other side

this is a puzzle not to be solved by Man, life's downside

Man is falsely satisfied by taking guesses at it and believing them

the secret will be kept a secret, at least as long as we remain on this side

Foolish Pride

how foolishly proud the rich man is of his wealth and assets

how hungry the wealthy runs for even more money with no regrets

look at the poor and the wealthy at the end of their journey of life

they go into the same ground, all the same decay and eaten up by the same maggots

Desireless

the hands of greed if cut, there is so little to desire

you're content with a loaf of bread, the day entire

truly he who is desireless, is always satisfied and free

greedy is always hungry for more and constantly in strife to acquire

Man's Plight

saw a Wiseman deep in thought

asked him if he knew the reason for Man's plight

he said, look at what we do and what we harbor in the heart

as long as enmity and hate is involved, days of Man will not be so bright

Friendship

let's build us a friendship as time is short

from the ship befriending the sea, there is a port

enmity and hatred do have an ugly face

O' what beautiful scenes are created with friendship of any sort

Pit of Darkness

how easy it is to fall into the pit of ignorance

how easy it is to stay in the darkness of stupidity and indifference

O' friend should you seek freedom from such tyranny

knowledge and wisdom will light the way to that realm
   of cognizance

All the Lies

oh the liar keeps misguiding all with his words

he thinks he has got his ship sailing towards safe shores

little he knows the lies are robbing him of many precious goals

in the end, whatever cover of humanity he has, sadly falls

Rain

O' raindrops fall on me and take away my sorrow

wish each drop could target my sadness like an arrow

indeed there is a message in every drop for all

O' Man, remove all darkness within, today and tomorrow

Life Without Hate

streams of hatred and greed in all of us abound

jealousy within is a giant, ugly and unsound

once removed with great will power, how merry life will be

love and friendship is then a pure wine of joy, for all around

Past Glory

as the beautiful flower wilts one day

youth and vitality will disappear without a say

what remains is you and all the dreams of yesterday

how that glorious past all of a sudden, became today

Changing Beliefs

your beliefs, whatever they may be

keep them to yourself, that's how it's meant to be

truly we change with time and so do our beliefs

be wise and live in peace with whoever you come to see

Ocean of Greed

our greed is like a deep ocean

all misery it brings, a toxic potion

if removed from the soul, though impossible it seems

all darkness in life disappears in a wands motion

Hidden Flaws

travel deep within your soul with open eyes

see all your flaws hidden in there, not one shape, not one size

as you gain a clear vision of all your imperfections inside

you'll see everyone a mirror of you wrapped in disguise

Prejudice

should roots of my prejudice dry away

all my demons within, like snow under the Sun will melt away

If one looks at everyone in the same light

only love and kindness is there to stay

Always There

you're not a friend if you come around for self-gain

you're not a friend if you only look for fun and no pain

a true friend is always there with you, no matter what the game

you're always safe around a true friend, again and again

Personal Story

we all live with our many memories of life

some good and some bad, all make up our personal story of strife

truly without such memories, life is meaningless at best

wish all we had were good memories where only happiness
   was rife

Oblivion

go alone to a cemetery and think hard

see all those gone before you, adult and child

there is nothing but destruction and nothingness to see around

when death knocks on your door, be content with the world of oblivion and discard

Light of Wisdom

keep quiet if you have no answers in mind

with no experience your knowledge needs to be refined

gain wisdom and learn to think things through

then see the world lighten up and life turn joyous and kind

The End Game

dark surprise in life is always around the corner

the bad news often comes with a coffin and a mourner

this is the real life, good and bad in a blender

just go slow and keep calm, the end game is always surrender

Rise Above

free your mind and thoughts so you can rise above

remove all the fears from the wrath of so-called god and feel the love

then see your life under a new light of wisdom

become a new person with a new vision you can be proud of

What I Know

I do not know from where I came to be

I do not know where I'll end up and what is there to see

all I know is that I am alive at this moment of time

not worried about the rest, let it be whatever it may be

Words and Jewels

words from the wise are those rarely found jewels

if you take them to heart, your life will be happy, unlike life of fool's

the fool also runs his mouth, far greater than the wise

his words are like trash strewn about, covering all the jewels

Dark Road

knowledge and wisdom are lights on a dark road of life

wherever they shine, darkness of the mind disappears with all its inherent strife

if they are lacking in a person, or worse, in a society

ignorance and blindness will be so thick you can't cut through with a knife

Peace

old age is sure a burden for Man, so profound

the more you see of the world, more sorrow there is to be found

lucky is the one who somehow finds peace and tranquility in life

without them, life is sinking into the ocean of grief with no rebound

Ignorance

ignorance is a deep stupor so dark and painful

it's a dragon with fiery breath of prejudice, so hurtful

O' Man root it out before it swallows you in whole

see how ignorance colors the world in sorrow and acts so shameful

No Borders

close your eyes and imagine no borders around

close your eyes and see happiness, everywhere to be found

sadly, all good is imagined only in our dreams these days

open your eyes again and see borders and regrets abound

Secret Potion

early morning woke up in a middle of a dream

thoughts all over the place, confusion extreme

in the narrow alleyways of wonder, searching for that secret potion of creation

hopeless and tired, settled back into the arms of sleep, O' life is once again calm and supreme

Aching Heart

O' my heart don't be saddened by this fleeting life

don't bother with youth passing you by and all the strife

God made you from a handful of dust and dirt

so you return to your origins, occurrence so rife

Life in Vain

all I grew in life withered away as autumn leaves

in the end it is me in the ground, so lonely it seems

O' young man take a look and learn this lesson of life

be wise for very soon whatever you sow, destiny reaps

Little Joys

my eyes you have seen much sorrow on this earth

ocean of sadness is around all of us from birth

days of joy and wine were there too, but so few in between

those little joys disappeared just too soon, and there was pain for Man to unearth

Mirror to the Soul

my prayers are mine, my personal possessions

they are a mirror to my soul and its reflections

O' friend, our deeds will sure return to us in various translations

we are the judge and the executioner of all our intentions

Deeds

extend your hand of kindness to all

not for a prize nor for boasting and looking tall

as you transform through your good deeds from inside out

then your world will change for good, before the curtains fall

Blind Devotion

religion is colored with hypocrisy and pain

devotion without knowledge is hollow with nothing to gain

O' Man, wakeup from your dark stupor

very soon you'll be placed into the ground, all your worshipping in vain

Coming to Disappear

truly we come to the world only to disappear

wine of joy in one hand how we struggle in life, oh dear

appreciate in full the little time you have on this earth

when we depart, our bodies only as dust will reappear

Pain of being Sober

give me a glass of wine and I'll gently dream away

all the good and the bad of this world, I'll sweep away

O' how Man suffers to the bone when he is sober

pour me another glass of wine and see the gentle breeze take me far, far away

Rain of Wisdom

there is truly no end to our ignorance and blindness

the unaware sees wielding a knife an act of kindness

the cure is standing under the rain of wisdom

what beautiful flowers grow in a wet soil far away from cold and darkness

Understanding

there are so many things in this world that I don't understand

many things that I think I do, but in reality misunderstand

one may ask, where in life do I stand?

my answer is simple, we are not given all the tools to know, such is the rule of this land

Nothingness

stepped into this world out of nothingness

went through the journey of life, some joy, much emptiness

now see the end of the road approaching fast

will have to leave and enter the world of lifelessness

Regrets

my old man whispered into my ear, just before he passed away

life is too flimsy, as you're witnessing today

be happy and make all around you happy too

when you get to this point, regret is a useless tool at the end of the day

Will

destiny has its ways of making us such fools

making us believe we have a will and all the essential tools

no one knows what wisdom lies behind this game of confusion

many ended up under the ground looking for answers, leaving us with no clues

Friends

O' friends, do come to my aid, this is a man so tired and hopeless

where has everybody gone, my life is soulless

if this loneliness continues, my days are sure to be even darker

what is life without friendship, an empty shell of a body, so ugly and formless

Hidden Faces

looked inside my soul, searching for my true face

amongst hundreds in there, so hard finding any trace

sadly, we all have many faces hidden inside

how I wish there was only one face, inside and out, and none of
   this disgrace

At the Heart

whatever you have at heart, it will show up in your actions

you think they are hidden, but all can see them in your reactions

so make things right at the source, dear friend

once your heart is cleansed, only beauty will rise in all your interactions

Masterful

O' how destiny plays games with us all

throws us up and then throws us down to fall

resist and struggle as much as you want

we are all losers at the end, at the hands of such masterful player we fall

Man and The Stars

think hard about the earth and all the stars above

think about all the secrets they hold and how everything fits like a glove

how much similarity can you find between them and all creatures on earth?

truly, there is a connection between those moving stars and flying of a dove

Inside

O' you who is always busy criticizing others

whose eyes are only looking out to find fault in his own brothers

look a little inside of you, search for your own reality

what misgivings are there to be found, one wonders

Art of Living

hey you, laying quietly in peace under the ground

some time has passed from all the noise you used to make, where is the sound?

you went and we all are in line to follow

guess we never learn the art of living till it is too late and we are no longer around

Wine from Heaven

O' my beautiful little child, welcome to my heart

you sat foot on this earth and lightened up my days with the joy you impart

hold my hand and I too become a child, no sorrow, no despair

truly you are my glass of wine from heavens to drink and get a new life from the start

The Only Hand

friendships are truly treasures far more precious than gold

a true friend is with you in the heat and in the cold

be aware not anyone at your corner is a friend

when trouble rises its ugly head, only the friend's hand is there to hold

Kindness

find a time to be alone, away from everyone, with your thoughts

bring forth all the good and the bad memories, all the silence, all the shouts

see through all the smoke and review your deeds, good and bad

in the end, you'll see the kindness you imparted will tower above all your faults

Life

if I only knew why I came to this world

the grief and sorrow would flyaway, so I am told

the world may look a bit kinder than it does now

On the other hand just maybe, that will make life even harder to bear and more cold

Fool's Logic

never argue with a fool, as it is like travelling on a road with no end

the fool is unaware of the reality, though likes to pretend

In fool's mind all he believes are set in stone, nothing to change

anything contrary to his belief, is to be fought with and condemned

Destiny's Game

destiny keeps playing games with us my friend

its tricks are mostly hidden till we get to the end

in our constant struggle with destiny through our flimsy life

we are always the loser, as we end up perished, with dirt to blend

Passengers

my heart, stop all that crying whenever you are sober

you will only live a short while, then it's all over

what are we but passengers on a fatal journey, no wonder

rejoice and be happy while you can, what is there to do
  but surrender

Old Age

how I ran so fast from my youth to my old age

passing through the mountains and valleys, one day so calm the other in rage

through this journey of confusion, saw signs of life all around me

sadly, as I looked further into the distance, there was only death on stage

Joy for All

prey all you want to any God you may have in desperation

it is the joy you impart which is the root of all aspiration

do not annoy or hurt your fellow man, do whatever your heart desires

the world is beautiful only when everyone has a share in jubilation

Changing World

all things will pass, bring me a glass of wine

maybe when I am drunk, I can see what is or isn't mine

this is an ever-changing world that stops for no one

we all are changing too, every second of the day, in this life we call divine

Wings of Wisdom

see the bird out of the cage as it soars into the sky

on top of the wind it goes higher and higher, yearns to fly

a man kept in the dark is that bird in the cage

with the wings of wisdom and the wind of thought, he soars higher and sees his powers multiply

Poor and Rich

I wonder what the wisdom is in our creation

some are given fortunes greater than our imagination

so many are poor and in need of a lifeline if just for a day

O' creator tell us, was our creation the result of a devilish temptation

Blindness

prejudice is a terrible disease of the mind

when you know we all come from one point and are of
   the same kind

humanity and kindness beautify all, no matter who and where

what then, makes a man so ignorant and terribly blind?

Power of Destiny

O' Man rejoice and be happy with this short life

like a piece of cake, destiny cut it out for you with its sharp knife

God is playing us in a game of chess right to the end

sadly, the winner is never us and we are always the one in strife

Man's Curiosity

O' creator what wonders you've done in Man's creation

though the doubt and confusion in life is far great to mention

wish curiosity wasn't one of Man's God given arsenals

this is the only fault in our narrative and God's dictation

Slave's Prayer

hey you, who is bending over a tomb praying to that so called holy grave

you cry and wail desperately seeking help, like a beggar or a slave

don't you know under that stone there is just more soil and dirt

truly wherever you step on this earth is as holy as that grave

Hollow Words

whatever said has to conform with what you do

oh how Man can run with words with no clue

be aware, words with no action are hollow and feel untrue

the wise sets his eyes on the actions of Man, like a glue

Autumn Winds

O' my love hold my hand till there is still time

pour me a glass of wine so pure and sublime

destiny will soon take everything off our hands

then there are autumn winds and withering away into slime

Faults

do not look for faults in everyone around

look within and see how many faults there are to be found

go deep and see if you can find any wisdom in your own deeds

cleanse your soul first, fault finding in others is an act so unsound

Picture on the Wall

as we depart this world on that lonely journey

nothing there to take, no toys, not a penny

those deeds of ours will still go on affecting some for a while

then all is left is an old picture on the wall looked at by few, if any

The Preacher

call me anything you like, I live my life on my own terms

I do refuse to feed off anyone on this earth like germs

O' so called man of God, whoever you are, stop preaching and leave me at peace

I despise those who sell faith for a living and make religion the most profitable of firms

Insignificance

we come to this world and soon away we depart

the secret is unknown to all, dumb or smart

through our flimsy life nothing is added or taken away from all the galaxies and the stars

for we are so insignificant a being, albeit such work of art

God's Mold

if destiny brings Man to this world

if God's wisdom takes him away, we are told

this coming and going is not of our own

just maybe, all evil and good in the world is cast in God's mold

Crying Man

Man cries as a baby as he steps into this world

this could be a sign there is no joy on this earth, some are told

as we depart, there is sorrow and cries again to behold

my friend, this coming and going is a sad story that never gets old

Love the Living

remember me while I am still breathing and alive

when bees are gone what's the use of building a hive

friendship and kindness are only for the living

under the ground we are only food for plants to thrive

Light of Life

from the autumn winds that mercilessly blow

see how perishable life is just like melting snow

from the yellow leaves falling onto the ground

be warned our light of life has limited time to glow

Generous Sun

I asked the sun, why do you shine so bright on all things around

offering your heat and light equally to all creatures on this ground

the sun replied, aren't we all created from a single source,
    O' mankind

prejudice is borne out of ignorance in those deep in the pool of
    selfishness, drowned

Last Wish

if you ask me, what is my last wish before I die

I'll tell you with no hesitation, in a short reply

all I have done in this world would be nothing to me in the end

just wish I could leave pleasant memories for all who will come
  for that last goodbye

My World

wish I just could be taken to another world

where there is no sorrow and no grudges to hold

all I see is happiness and kindness around

I am aware of why I came to be and why I will be taken away,
   as I am told

Speck of Dust

in a dream saw myself flying in space

from afar could barely find our earth or any of its trace

said to myself, wow, that speck of dust is what we all embrace

suddenly woke up, there was that great wonder and confusion for me to face

Joy of Others

what is better in life than making someone happy

giving a hand of help, bringing joy to others aplenty

what is better than changing a crying face into a smiling one

picking up a fallen man and set him on his way, filling a life that was so empty

Life and Death

fallen leaves in the autumn breeze, are death displayed in beautiful colors

death as life, can well be appealing for us and the others

what we do see and feel is important, not what is actually happening in front of us

truly, interpretations of life and death vary from us to the others

Imagination

asked a wise man if he knows anything from the other side

he said what we know about it are only our imaginations we build inside

things you've not experienced in reality are only tricks of the mind

as we leave this life, all our tools of imagination are gone to the wayside

Selfish Man

tired of knocking on closed doors all the time

selfishly all I wanted was for my own good in my lifetime

wasn't aware we humans are all connected as links in a chain

any force applied upon the chain will affect all the links, a reality so sublime

Different God

if I were God, would have created Man differently

would have given him great logic housed in a brain separately

would have given him less greed and more wisdom
  and contentment

my creation would know why he is brought to life for this little
  time, then taken away indefinitely

Clues

always searching for answers from any source of wisdom that I can find

hoping to find any clues to the puzzle of Man so lost, though a creature so refined

as many before, so tired of looking and circling around

well aware that I will depart this world and the answer will never be found

Struggle

beside a little lake, a fish had fallen out onto the dry land

struggling for life, looking for any help at hand

the scene reminded me of Man's struggle in his daily existence

except that the fish fights for dear life, and Man for more power and his reign to expand

Darkness

goodness will never bear fruit in a ground covered with ignorance

instead, you'll see darkness of prejudice grow there in abundance

must till the ground real deep to have air of wisdom flow through

if not, all you have is misery, sorrow and indifference

Destiny

sat in a room, quietly drowned in my thoughts

going through my life's pathway, seeing all the good and
 all the faults

tried to understand which acts were truly of my own volition

concluded sadly, they were all acts of destiny on display, finally
 connected the dots

Pure Joy

happiness of a child, how pure and pleasant it feels

the child lives in the moment, no worries, just dreams

as we grow old, that purity is well gone and forgotten

maybe because we are constantly scared of the past or the future of our schemes

Dearly Departed

the departed are taken from us, there is no news

we just hope they are somewhere safe, paying their dues

don't bother searching for the truth of the afterlife, dear friend

just hope you'll find it out on the other side, where life as we are told continues

Gone

without you there is no more laughter, no more joy

shadows everywhere, no more light of day to enjoy

pity you are gone forever, never coming back

just wonder who is behind all this tragedy, or is this just a ploy?

My Eyes

these eyes have seen much sorrow and despair

in this world, much darkness and tragedies in the air

only if there was some wisdom in what we humans do

there would be relief and tranquility into which our eyes stare

Last Grasp

like it or not, this life will escape the grasp of your hands

your connection to this world will end, as it stands

you will return to the dark earth once again

after that, seems there was never anyone like you walking the lands

Our Dust

shaking the dust off my clothes I began to wonder

within all the dust, see the remnants of the past king's and
  queen's splendor

truly we all will become dust one by one

whose clothes will Harbor our dust, I began to ponder

Secrets of Creation

dreamt of finding God's treasure trove of creation

in it, found all the hidden secrets of his operation

filled with joy that I now know the purpose for our existence

suddenly woke up, forgetting all the unveiling, back to my frail imagination

End of Life

all that youth and excitement are gone now, so far away

all that joy and sorrow of life went by, seems in a single day

look how calm and serene you are being laid into the ground

thousands of hopes and arguments vanished, nothingness to stay

Giving Life

see the Sun shining bright at a distance

in that ball of fire there is light and heat in every instance

with generosity and kindness, it bestows life on everything around

no prejudice at all, shines equally on all with unwavering persistence

Purpose

dazed and confused at this strange life of mine

hurt and feel abused by facing non-existence at a certain time

wish I knew who is going through all this trouble of building and destroying

wish I just knew if there is any purpose to all these acts of crime

Greed

amazed at the one who seeks evermore wealth and power

greedy, he strives to take things away from the other

doesn't he know life passes by quick, as winter and spring

doesn't he know he will leave all for others to take or plunder

Aimless

look deep at those sleeping departed under the ground

then see how many living who are asleep, there are to be found

Man goes on living in an aimless circle of life

pity, there is no help from anyone or anything around

Dark Journey

I was born on a cloudy day just like today

almighty gave me life, though I didn't ask for, guess it was kindness on display

took me through my journey of life up to this point, my gratitude

pity, at the end as at the beginning, I will be in the dark, to my dismay

Puzzle of Life

as we come and go through this life

there is just misery and destruction and a whole lot of strife

if that mighty creator had a purpose for his plans

that will remain a puzzle, not to be solved in this life

The Promise

Oh please, someone tell me what Man is to do on this speck of dust

what is creation for and why are we living this life that we must

we know we will leave as we came, in confusion and bewildered

why is there a promise of heaven for this lost being who eventually turns into dust

The Wise

asked a wise man on a lonely road

how do you tell apart the wise from a fool, let the truth be told

he said the fool runs his mouth about anything in the world

the wise mostly keeps quiet, listening to what's being told

Words

speaking is like water flowing through a canal

if harsh, as overflowing water, will damage and destroy, no rationale

spend a little thought before uttering your words

this is the way of the wise who live in harmony with their high morale

Actions

all our actions originate at first in the mind

so our deeds are to be looked at under a light refined

our hands are not the creator of our actions be warned

question is, what controls the mind, the answer so hard to find

Actions and Thoughts

he whose actions and thoughts are both on the path of good is truly free

when on a path of harm, there is madness and trouble for all to see

one who talks the talk, but doesn't walk the walk is a hypocrite

in the end he will wither away in misery, like a rotten tree

Memories

O' friend where did all that friendship and joy go

how time built a wall between us, became a foe

though we are now both covered with all that grey hair and sorrow

many pleasant memories of you still color my mind, hope you know

Last Day

never know when your last day will come, the end of your empire

never know where your last breath will leave you to expire

therefore, wherever you go, be mindful and treasure the moment

maybe just there and then, is your last experience of life entire

Awakened Mind

ignorance is sometimes a sorry state of pleasure

when aware, those nasty questions come around, taking you on a sad adventure

going back to sleep and that state of oblivion is a way out of misery indeed

a mind awake is a terrible burden, though it is part of human nature

Divided

ignorance has divided Man into hundreds of sects

each has a god of his own no one else respects

the almighty isn't any help in solving the problem at all

humanity goes on bewildered and confused with so many regrets

Life of a Bubble

life is analogous to a bubble riding on the water

in one look it seems strong, sitting on the waves, no bother

casually it goes on a journey, in search of something new

suddenly, with one tiny flick, the bubble disappears into the body of its mother

Secrets

fate has mysterious ways of expression

you can guess all you want and try to be a magician

the secrets of this life are hidden to all

just hang on a bit, all curtains fall when we turn into
an exhibition

Lonely Journey

the spring of life turns into winter, just too soon

all you've possessed is taken from your hands all in tune

it's only you in that lonely journey of death

what remains for only a while, are bones in the ground, under the lonely moon

Troubled Heart

this heart of mine, how I want to run from you in despair

with you at my side, this life is in a state of disrepair

all I see from you is drunkenness and destruction

wish I knew what the remedy is to this state so unfair

Friend Indeed

O' friend I feel your absence with all my heart

in all the hassles of everyday life, your presence was unique, like a work of art

with you my life would have been calm and free of any sorrows

a true friend fills your heart with joy and with him, all despair and anguish depart

Autumn of Life

seeing the grey hair in the mirror in the autumn of life

a signal that the end of the road is near, scary as
 an approaching knife

alas, we only go through this journey of life this once

lets live it up then, no use in regretting all the bad and all
 the strife

To the Creator

if I ever get to see that mighty creator of ours

have lots of complaining to do for all the tears in our eyes

what was the wisdom in giving us life on this earth for this short while?

after much sorrow, returning us back to the dust we once were on the stars

Fear of Life

I do not fear death and nothingness

I do fear this fragile life and so called happiness

the former, you are no longer alive to feel any fear

the latter, you are alive but filled with fear and emptiness

In Due Time

O' friend you know we will only last a short time

get your horse saddled, there is a mountain to climb

death is just around the corner, always a surprise

there is no escape, we all will be in its clutches in due time

Man in the Frame

looked at a picture frame, me in it from my younger days

for all that I have lost, felt like hell to raise

how quick all went by in a blink of an eye

just about to settle in life, must prepare for that dreaded world of decays

At Peace

see how all the mayhem and hassles of life are gone

see how all the laughter and sorrow got passed on

how peaceful you are now laying in the ground

see how there are no more promises or hopes to lean on

Last Kiss

saw a beautiful flower, a pedestal to a pretty butterfly

the fly kept kissing the flower with a gentle cry

few days passed and I came across that scene again

destiny left nothing of the flower, just a broken wing of the fly

Death

what are we, just a prey for that eagle of death

nowhere to hide, just wait for your last breath

think a little, where and how did we come to life

maybe that eagle of death is part of life in stealth

Taking Action

sorrow is all around, smell it in the air

see the hands go up in prayer and despair

so long is the wait for any help, but none is coming

O' Man stand up and take action, prayers alone are no help, beware

The Plan

bring me a glass of wine, oh you wise man

pour all the secrets of creation in it if you can

will drink it all and become filled with joy

just may be that haunting puzzle of life will be solved by this plan

House of Dirt

see the departed quietly resting in a house of dirt

along with all the others who went before us and left us hurt

strange, we all are creatures of dirt by origin

still puzzled when we are returned back to our roots, with death to flirt

True Friend

a true friend is the one when you're in need

stands beside you ready to help indeed

he does things for you to relieve and remedy

his time is yours, there is never any need to plead

Actions and Prayers

said to me a wise friend one day

you know Man is mighty strange in life and in play

at night his cries and prayers for mercy are always on display

then he goes on waging war on others for a penny, just the next day

New World

had a dream of a world with no borders

wherever I went there was a home in all corners

all I saw were friends living in peace as brothers

hands of friendship and help were all around, no mourners

Teaching by Action

O' friend practice what you preach

what you do leaves an imprint far greater than any speech

with no wisdom, there is nothing but empty words

He who has wisdom, there's a world to reach

www.ingramcontent.com/pod-product-compliance
Lightning Source LLC
Chambersburg PA
CBHW062226080426
42734CB00010B/2043